Guarding the Flame
MAJELLA CULLINANE

salmonpoetry

Published in 2011 by
Salmon Poetry
Cliffs of Moher, County Clare, Ireland
Website: www.salmonpoetry.com
Email: info@salmonpoetry.com

Copyright © Majella Cullinane 2011

ISBN 978-1-907056-79-6

All rights reserved. No part of this publication may be reproduced or transmitted in any form or by any means, electronic or mechanical, including photography, recording, or any information storage or retrieval system, without permission in writing from the publisher. The book is sold subject to the condition that it shall not, by way of trade or otherwise, be lent, resold or otherwise circulated without the publisher's prior consent in any form of binding or cover other than that in which it is published and without a similar condition, including this condition, being imposed on the subsequent purchaser.

COVER PAINTING: *'Pohutukawa Abstract"*, acrylic on canvas, by Harold Coop, Auckland, New Zealand
COVER DESIGN: *Siobhán Hutson*

Salmon Poetry receives financial support from The Arts Council

For Andrew

Acknowledgements

Acknowledgements are due to the editors of the following publications where several of these poems have appeared: *Crannóg Literary Magazine, The Sunday Tribune, The Stinging Fly, Stolen Weather: St. Andrews University Chapbook, Southword, The SHOp, JAAM, The International Literary Quarterly, Takahe, Poetry New Zealand,* and *Blackmail Press.*

The author gratefully acknowledges receipt of an Irish Arts Council Training and Professional Development Award in 2005, a Scottish Arts Council Creative Writing Fellowship from Aberdeen City Council in 2006, and a writer's residency in Achill from the Heinrich Böll Association in 2008. Thanks are also due to Harold Coop who kindly permitted the use of his painting 'Pohutukawa Abstract' as a cover.

Contents

Butterfly	11
Last Seen	12
Poem in February	13
Farfalle	14
Insomnia	15
Cold Snap	16
Nepalese Meditations	17
Pohutukawa	18
Achill	19
The Red Petticoat	20
Not So Far Behind	21
Swimmer	22
A Distant Shore	24
Autumn Is Where You Find It	25
Ruru	26
The Force of Things	27
Homecoming	29
Leaves	30
Emigrants	31
Orcadian Lament	32
At Bay	33
Night Porter	34
Heartbeat	35
Papago's Promise	36
Crossovers	37
Dream	38

The Quickening	39
Glenmore St	40
Birdling's Flat	41
A Wife's Promise	42
April	43
Morning Prayer	44
Memory of Birds	45
The Small Hours	46
Autumn's End	47
Niamh	48
A January Evening	49
Sionna	50
Paekakariki	51
Kiss	52
Quest	53
Virago	54
How To Find A Way	55
Bolton St. Memorial Park	56
Year of Our Lord, 1675	57
Knead	58
Solstice	60
Desert Road	61
Guarding the Flame	62
Nora and Jim	63
Rooms	64
Notes	67
About the Author	69

Butterfly

Only to say the thought comes
on a winter's morning, at a train station.
The sky an ashen blue, reeds murmur
behind a track, a bark tails a car
driving past. You wonder about it then,
how to explain the butterflies you've seen,
fluttering around music halls, their image
waving high on a kite, and again
at the end of glass stems in a shop display.
It occurs to you then –
the brush of your cheek on my face
is like a butterfly wing.

Last Seen

> *A strong wind… actually could enter you…*
> *and sometimes you get the feeling of having*
> *lost your bearings.*
>   TED HUGHES

No way to guess how a barred window
might be a grace —

against a storm slashing
the sky with twisted light,
thunder roaring like artillery lines.

Cursive rain assaults the street,
barges into barrios where women
in protest beat pots and pans.

There goes the fish market
through the air, past the last-minute
rush of kids selling their wares,
before it really strikes,

a wind last seen, sliding its forked tongue
through a net, tugged at my chest,
tightening a bolt there, just an inch —

until there is no way to say

we have not taken shape somewhere else.

Poem in February

    Here
snow skies and frost. Last night
I glanced up,
saw an assembly of seagulls settle
    on a station roof,
heard young Goths with Cleopatra eyes
make commotion
as I waited for a train to arrive.

There,
blue skies, windmills dotted for miles,
    the quixotic territory of love.
The ocean was too far from our centre –
    a mattress on a marble floor,
the incense-filled air, the woman downstairs
    singing
  as she hung out clothes.

Once
    I conjured orange trees
on Andalusian roads,
tried to interpret our future
    in the echo of cobbled stones
    and there I heard it –
love like the silent letter
    at the end of a word.

Farfalle

> *"It"s astounding how little the ordinary person notices butterflies."*
>   Nabokov

Even so, the not-so-ordinary person might watch
butterflies kissing the drowsy cheek of a flower
as clouds shed their cares in a murmur of rain.

Insomnia

You are there again,
cast amid the flotsam and tangle of a wave.
In the half-pitch, pitch darkness of the shore,
the sea is tinged and flecked with cloud and rain.

The Monarchs on your breastbone,
awake, awake and take to the air. You hear
their wings through the tip-top tumble of sand,
and as if to keep dawn forever at arms length

the night moves inside the house again.
Shadows wait outside the door,
and dreams rattle against windowpanes,
they want in, want in.

Inside the room
your breaths are like a crumpled sheet, folded,
or the hushed silence heard through a seashell
washed up on a beach. Open your mouth

taste the sand, the silence
loosened inside your dreams, the wrapped
sheets of your longing softening your skin.

When blackbird wings flicker
beneath your eyelids, you'll know you're awake.

Cold Snap
for my mother

That night when white-silked ice spread through fields
I imagined frozen blackberries and daffodils.
Outside the sky was charged with snow
and not unwelcome, the cold paced the room,
an exotic animal panting feathery blue.

What did you dream that starched night
when across the road traffic lights, ticked, ticked
green, amber, red,
and the earth held warmth at bay
like the frozen air, too astonished. They say
the Inuit have a dozen or so words for snow and ice –
all that cannot be held must acquiesce,
and yet not your careful hands tucking me in,
for it is that which still warms me.

Nepalese Meditations

Children are calico clouds
    echoing Namaste namaste.

The high-pitch rattle of women sifting rice
    on a roof moves through evening.

As we sleep the wind parcels stones
    over corrugated roofs like monks chanting Om.

The breathing dreams of the valley gleam
    amid tendril clouds of coral-mauve.

A star winks over Hillary's step.

Between a stupa and dhoka red-tongued dragons
    lash out at the monastery gate
where not even the reflection of a half-moon
    would dare transgress.

Pohutukawa

Suppose I ask of you
cliff-dweller,
what you make of me
walking this clover grass,
tasting the salty
periwinkles of another
hemisphere
in my mouth?

Achill

I

Listen to the wind slip secrets
through the heather-hued hills —
what does it say for blue-indigo
longing gathered in clouds,
the touch of a wave
where two tides converge?

II

In a house, the pages of the day's
conversation are flicked by flame,
charred by turf
until there is nothing left
but the rupture of smoke
trawling an empty road.

The Red Petticoat

> *In 19th century Ireland, the differences in dress between the middle-class lady and the poor woman were dramatic.*
>   'Dress in Ireland,' DELANEY

I can't say why
only as I followed her through the market
I imagined myself as her, held

her wicker basket on the hook of my arm,
felt my buckled toes spread in her wide, flat brogues.
I could have sworn

my ribs fell to my feet for when I looked
I saw two large breasts unfettered – a life of their own.

I heard the broad vowels of her dialect in my mouth
as I held loins of meat to the light,
examining for freshness, bargaining for price.

I was almost fully formed, enjoying the warmth
of her petticoat spread on my thighs

when sensing me behind she turned,
something circumspect in her peasant face.
Pardon me Mam she said.

It was my own voice I heard then.

All at once I felt a tightness loop around my waist,
my skin drew back as I inhaled
each corseted breath slowly as I had for years.

Nothing left of my change or so I thought
until
        later
the red of that petticoat
burnt in my dreams like a scar.

Not So Far Behind

When distance was as miniature
as a night sky held by a window
and nothing seemed as concrete
as your curved fingers,
or the brown of your eyes

I had long before set out,
left the enclosure of your walls,
the rows of china tiered
like a pagoda in the living room,
the sound of drawers opening
as you looked for keys,

and who would have guessed
I'd find myself here,
the same age they say Christ died
walking up a drive,
no Plough in the Stars
to chart in this southern sky,

the light fading
as I pass the orchard,
a morepork watching me as I walk,
the moonlight
carrying your dreams a day behind.

Swimmer

Sometimes
I forget –
then a twinge,
a niggling,
two distinct
movements
of elbow and arm
as you stroke
fishbone clouds
of dark-
swaddled womb –
my intrepid
swimmer.

I have no image
of you;
as hard-pressed
as the moon
searching
for her face
in sloe-
eyed waves,
or a shadow
pushed aside
by white light.

In the shift
of bones
you carve
an inlet,
weave and dive
through
muffled caves.

Each day
the light there
grows
deeper, wider
like pockets
of dreams
folded out,
checked
and brimming.

A Distant Shore

Inside her dress pocket, black beads rattle
as she walks the clover-covered hill,
past the creek that meets the sand, the driftwood,
the shade of a Pohutukawa tree.
She walks the shore,
and as if setting down kindling for twilight,
takes the beads from her pocket,
sparks the air with prayer.
Words meet her teeth and tongue, return to her,
replete with waves, salty and wet.
Between amens and the Coromandel,
she is taken over tides, through the warm air of summer,
back to mist-coloured hills, different trees, older ones,
an older world.

She rubs the glass beads between a finger and thumb –
the act of touching an incantation,
new sounds tripped from hearing. Home again,
home. No more fuss from kakas
parading the trees in crimson collars and dark-edge feathers,
no rain on a corrugated iron roof, tap, tapping into her heart.
An old heart map she clings to,
bays and inlets from another hemisphere impressed there.
She does not hear in those breezes,
the coiling whispers of oceans that come here
as she does each night, uninvited,
as stubborn as her in their devotion.

Autumn Is Where You Find It

Early morning. Light washes over Aotea square
and as I walk I hear the sounds of China,
watch as a small group gathered there
moves to the measured grace of Tai Chi Chuan.

How like the season, that fluid falling away
the rise of a hand, or foot, the way the body turns,
each gesture heightening the red-orange leaves
of the non-native tree standing behind them.

Further on a Polynesian woman feeds some birds
and the dark scripted shop signs in Korean
remind me of waking earlier in semi-darkness.
From the kitchen window I watched as mists drifted
and stretched over hills, and with each moment
cloud maps over the sky resisted constancy.

Ruru

Let me tell you
a bed-time story
echoed as it is,
again and again,

    sifted and plotted
through the creek of trees
where
the cicadas grow faint,

and a fleck of feathers
begins to stir,
fierce eyes alert,
yet conciliatory.

You would not be wrong,
    owl guardian
of the half-light,
there is something that resists
an end,

that stalks the last lines
of a story.

I listen to distance,
to your cries nestled
in the hollow of a tree,
or high up on a branch

repeating
words of warning,

advice, advice.

But who are you telling?
the wind, the dark?

Not so much grace
for prey,
the need in you
splintered now
as you banquet on weta,
beetle, moth.

And not one of us
can tell how it will end,
only

the light, the light.

The Force of Things

I have tapped the arch of the scapula
    where the skin dips
to the breastbone.

Your breaths
    are the quivering feathers
    of birds
rustling eucalyptus, macrocarpa, pine.

It's a question of listening:

the guttural call of your dreams
    a kind of offering
I nestle in the cup of my hands.

    I snatch the ghost of things
    you cannot see.

It is this that frightens you.

    The wind holds its blade
against the night's throat,
but like you, it too will soon forget –

the taste of my lips
    buoyed in a gully of dreams.

Homecoming

When clouds gush conversations through windows,
and the fricative song of the cicada gives way to twilight
take the gravel path down the hill, past the orchard
heavy with apples, apricots, plums, through the passage.
Out there the hours are gathering for what is lost
in the liquid chime of tuis scuttling the air, kauri
stretching its spine to scoop the first sight of stars.

Any night now the shattered glass of the greenhouse
will dislodge itself and blaze across the wind,
cutting the air to pieces. But you wanted to say it straight,
talk your way out of unbelonging, whisper yourself
into the leaves, the branches, the bark of a familiar pine,
to the the call of birds flying northward.

Leaves

Nothing like you
stands out at dusk.

I gathered you then
as I walked a path,
thousands
of your siblings
around me,
crushed and wet.

I had watched closely,
hoping you might fall
into my hands by chance,
or crackle a greeting
as you swept the road.

Looking at your lines,
your veins
burnished for change,
I thought none of us
could have known
when you might slip
from a branch
and wind-tossed,
find me there.

Emigrants
for my father

It made them wonder if it were true —
that rumour across the sea —
you could earn a year's wage in one month,
collect it in an orderly line,
send part of it home.

It made them feel wrong in themselves,
those mocking orders falling thick in frost and fog,
branded outsider for the beat of their tongue.

It made them seek relief in dance halls,
in the barrel of a glass where
only the wooden eye of a table stared back.

It made the soles of their feet hurt,
reeling and jigging their way back
to leaking barns, ditches and hills
where love rolled and thrust
from hips and mouths.

They believed they were fools — all of them
leaving the tabernacle of youth knowing only
the length of one street, a town square, a monument
inspired by war, a stone hero pointing a rifle in the air,
holding the dead captive in the churchyard.

Orcadian Lament

He would hold the comb carefully
just as he might a small injured bird,
his fingers tense for friction, resistance
as he'd unravel the long rope of hair.

He loves that sound –
when she teases the snarls out –
in it he hears the rigging of a boat,
waves against the prow,
the slow rhythm of oars stroking the sea.

Leave the work of dreams to darkness,
the gold of the day coming down in shadows
is what he attends to.

A strange creature this woman,
as much like the riddle of stones they passed today,
those stationary warriors to wind,
their armour lichen-licked,
damp-inhaled with snow and sea.

The glint in her hair then
as the air turned oyster-grey,
and trees were crushed with ice and snow.

From nowhere,
a warmth in his veins, on his beard
and tongue he tasted ice,
swallowed the words
he cannot bring himself to say –
Woman, hand me that comb.

At Bay

How long we stood there is anyone's guess,
as long as twilight on the horizon's edge, or waves
sluicing their bodies on wind-cuffed rocks,
longer yet to darken the powdery blue of your eyes,
the hours closing down for night. We did not look back
as we walked through vanilla-scented grass,
our bearings remembered by the moon's mild eye,
the impromptu stir of nikau palms shed.
Later as you slept I kept watch, the small window
concealing the moon in a mask of cloud. Listening
to your breaths, the scuttle of rats in the puriri joists,
the edges of morning at first diminutive, softened
and spread. It had been this I had waited for
like the traveller just returned, asking for news of kin.

Night Porter

There would be the ritual ironing
of your shirt
and knotting of your tie
before you would start
and slip your cracked feet
into the tailored soles of night

and drift to the beep
pulsing at your hip
calling you to hold down some drunk
while another poured charcoal
down their throat,
or push a trolley to the morgue.

I would not notice
you were gone
until you came in the next day
from a twelve-hour shift.
I'd hear you climb the stairs,
my mother's voice and then I'd drift back
to dream. It was only there
I'd see you, among white curtains
and syringes and visitors buying comfort
from news stands and flower displays.

Heartbeat

I

It was Ariadne
who spun a thread to guide Theseus out.
I too chart your advance, watch the flutter
of your heartbeat on a spectral screen –
the curve of you like a tiny moon
propped on the hammock of a night sky.

II

There might be something in it –
opening a fraction, listening to sound gather
as if through a mollusc, less the wind,
more the echo of blood pulsing in the ear,
blood catching up on itself, meshed
and criss-crossed in the furrow of our bones.

III

You wander the interior
veered by stroke-spell, the light blurred
and shifting as you roll and bend.

IV

Who would have guessed
sunlight to nudge us on –

as insistent, hear it,
    leaf-sound trickling the air.

Papago's Promise

    Bring me colour,
coppery sunlight, mottled sun-stain,
the olive gloss of tear-shaped leaves, satin-soft,
trickling breezes of water in a brook;
    the crackling wood just born,
and later in the season, the parched
leaves severed from their parents,
wandering forest trails lost and alone.
    Don't forget flowers,
petals of light crimson,
velvet fuchsia, citrus amber,
    and sky – bluish-grey, opal-azure,
tawny sunsets from shape-shifter clouds,
    metallic rain.
I will add texture, shape:
    bands, dots, spangles,
carve my new creatures' wings
from my children's
    dappled dreamscapes.
When I finish, they open my bag –
their ruby ringlets of laughter rising
    as they watch butterflies
escape into the sun, the leaves,
the flowers, the sky.
    It is they who name them:
painted lady, monarch, morning cloak,
swallow tail, leopard lacewing, karner blue.
    Only the sun
    being the star she is, and
    too quick to ignite,
folds her coppery tongue
    in envy and does not speak.

Crossovers

I

If I were to name it, or better
ask the season to hold what I cannot –
what might it be?
Moonlight through a silver birch,
the smoky-blue gatherings of night
as the small hours forage for light.

II

The day breathes in and out
and in what is shed
there is opportunity – a shift
as subtle as coral pink clouds
gathering behind trees on a hill.

III

In the hush of cold waves
I could enter myself
until there was no sound but one breath.

We could lay down, and be for each other
pilgrims of inconstancy. One wave,
then another, a perfect syntax,
as rhythmical as a dance starting up.

What presses through the stillness –
an emptiness I could fall into.

Dream

We sleep in each other's keeping
and if we find a trace of blue sky
this winter morning we'll take it as a gift
just as the dream you remember now,
of waking to find a child sleeping
between us in the bed. So it is again,

morning is the mistress of beginnings.
Outside the blackbird struts the undergrowth
for worms, the black fern canopies
the clothes line. Downstairs,
the clink of your spoon against a bowl
echoes the rain's tapping song.

The Quickening

    Just as a wave
must give itself to the absoluteness of release

so it is with you, this quickening –
    as much like
a stone skittered on the surface of a stream,
    a small fish breaking through a wave.

As stars blaze and burrow in a wild spring night
      I hold fast to this room, to this bed,

the mattress beneath me, the frame intact.
    I am like the balance weighed down by gold –

for it is you who has upended me.

Glenmore St

When the rain swallows the sky's colour,
    like a rogue sea thrown off course
one shift

of tectonic plates here or there
    and the colonial houses behind us
might tumble down the terraced hills

  make our walls tremble,
the lampshades a little more than nervous.

Last minute, I could take it all in –
    what I've done
to make this small house home:

the Kashmiri rug from the Fair Trade shop;
    two Indian mats that drift
    across the floor,
an African violet no longer in bloom.

Nothing here of beginnings,
of extraction, or nation; the curled fern frond
on the deck as unconvinced as I. So

when the rain clears, and the carnage of place
    has digressed farther from its point, I'll return again

to this window for now, to the view
    of feathered clouds clearing
    a rain-soaked sky.

Birdling's Flat

In the hour changed over tonight
more than light has been saved, put behind:
the handful of stones we held in our hands,
the dampness of waves concealed
beneath layers of shingle beach.

Could the sea have heard our pledge then,
repeated later in a borrowed room
where light had fled into walls and ceilings
and shadows stood at the doors of dreams
opening; attendant to the inconstancy
of colour amid tussock, to the wild daisies
of orange and pink pushing through.

A Wife's Promise

Given the chance,
he would question the mirror
about the bruise and blood on his cheek.

While he sleeps,
she binds his hands and legs,
watches the fall of snow
as it holds stillness on the street.
She closes the door to another day
clenching its fist outside.

She has lost count
of knuckle prints on her skin,
She is a bruised crocus,
the pocketful of ashes in a ring-a-rosy rhyme.

She hears children play outside,
music stream down
from the butcher's, the draper's,
the ocean that brought her here.

The snow has stopped now.
As she watches the knife reflect on his neck,
she holds it there
like a pendulum, a promise, a charm.

April

Take it in –
close hills circling the harbour,
a blue sky simple in suggestion,

jade-light behind trees,
where children meander
jigsaws of laughter.

At the gates of the graveyard
a lone tui rests
atop a half-stripped birch
and does what it must –
flies away.

Morning Prayer
after Tchaikovsky

Half-way through your journey you are called out.
From the dimmed room of your making, we watch

you moving like a corridor of shadows across a sea,
or the cool fingers of autumn stroking a tree.

Your small hand flexes and tightens, your spine
curves against me like a horseshoe, a strung bow.

The brazen scarlet of a gum tree fades on the hill
and like the season, it is still early days for you and me;

for my bones to soften, my body to swell. Wait
for me in the undertow of waves. It is there

I will catch you my little boy, and when
you emerge we can explore the novelties of light.

Memory of Birds

The ancient magic
of bird song
skirts the cool air,
a sketchy sense of direction
in the stunned half-light
of early autumn.
The silver birch
is emptying
for the waxeye
and its green-glinted eye,
for the fantail
fluttering hieroglyphs
with its fancy tail.

Not far from here
the cormorant glides
above a tryst of sea
and stream.
All I can take of this or that
the heart might unfeather –
like the cracked shell
of a mussel
I held in my hand once,
the colour
of a magpie wing.

The Small Hours

Had I been berthed in the abbreviated hush of night
or coerced by some inchoate navigator
to the chance landing without telescope or map,
I might have deciphered shadow and landmark,
but nothing now constrains this shift of flesh and bone
the thought of you is never far from me,
returning as though a missive to this small room.

My ears are cocked for the solitary chant
of the morepork, the anguished howl of a stranger
echoed on the road. I count on breaths
to draw me back to this morning's hard-pressed rain.

Before I come to fully, give me a moment
in the cloistered room of memory where my father
is Vulcan carrying a coal scuttle in, lining the fire
with deliberate ritual: branches are cracked and split,
a newspaper ripped and twisted, a match struck.

In the smoke rising there like incantation
of crisp blue air, lifting out from itself, the interior
of flame is the matador's cloak enticing a charge,
just as in this room now shadows are charged with light,
and the rain that would drench the skin damp,
will later arouse the blood to warmth and glow.

Autumn's End

I

The simple blueness of sky speaks for itself:
autumn – with its unique lilt
slips through the morning air.

II

I can't help but wonder
how long it will last
before what has become a comfort
will be upended by southerly winds;
the bones of the house shaken
by winter's Voodoo priest.

Niamh

How did I find myself here
among shadow-dancing leaves,
where trees whisper secrets
I do not understand.

I see a man,
his journey to battle,
a crow's feather drifting
in the arms of a breeze.
There is blood on his limbs.

I knew him once, or so I think.
Perhaps I dressed his body
with a duty that turned to love.

Absence paints twilight –
vermilion, elderberry, indigo, cream.

It occurs to me then, perhaps
I am here to interpret
the semantics of grief.

A January Evening

The perennial on the lawn
grows taller,
tantalising
naked trees
like upturned brooms
on the green
with its full branches.

The sky
grows a feverish violet
and settles into evening.

Birds perform their finale
as street lights turn on.

Some would say
there's snow
in the air,
but it isn't cold enough.

Sionna

I have sensed movement,
not in her current
as she shifts under Thomond,
or at the lush borders of her bank
where she echoes her dark song back to herself,
but in the distant flow of seas
parted by her curved corridor.

Losing sight of east and west,
I am brought back here
where a scimitar of light draws down
and a grey mist trickles over her.

She forages for silence behind walls
trying to forget the rupture
of lost battles and severed bones.
Like slate and dolomite,
she runs over features,
charts veins like a compass,
pulls memory down
as the rain greets the Atlantic.

Only in the east, thrown by tides
can I escape, leave her to a platform
of stars who remember the day
she leaned over waters to gather hazelnuts;
inside each the secret of verse.

As the nuts fell,
erupting into a deep purple,
the waters rose in anger
and carrying her away howled Sionna.

Paekakariki

It would take all there is to return,
to startle the fading eyelids of the day,
the powdery grey insistence of night coming in,
tinged and waiting atop the trees,
to re-imagine the shimmer of waves
of an earlier hour. I could liken the touch
of a petal to the soft lobe of an ear,
listen to the element of sound caught,
rendered in a single stroke, or in the quicksilver
glance, the shattered driftwood
thrown up by a storm, waves criss-crossing
patterns on the exhausted shore. Whatever
comes to mind as I lean a fist on my cheek,
an elbow through the breached heart of a book;
it is from there, the mustiness of pages rises
just as the salt air drifts across the beach,
to the crush of shells snagged on our feet,
the loose scattering of midden along a dune flank,
revealed — the chance feather, the peppery grey stone
of a past generation still warm in our hands.

The Kiss

So much of ourselves scattered
in the weightlessness of touch.

Outside trees take deep breaths,
clothes on a line grieve for bodies
they will never own.

Inside the soft kiss you gave me
grows a second skin.

Quest

It is the light we seek, not so much
of the apostle or faithful follower
but simpler –
in a small garden
we could find it transfigured
by the diminutive –
the flower petal coaxed by a bee,
a bird's wing strumming a leaf.

Virago

Stretching the walk out of her legs,
she cupped an apron bearing food;
the moving rock of her, abundant, solid —

gathered like thirst under her tongue
as she turned bends, already familiar
with the myth of the road,
its developing narrative.

Calming its momentum, her eyes
introduced an ensemble of rusted gates,
a cow straying

through sorrel, a lintel of clouds
at the skull of a hill she mounted
with ankle boots and woollen socks.

Boughs plaited by wind and rain cave
to the buttress of her
as they traced her steps
down the same ground decades before
when a hunger not forgotten brought
her off the road,
to a hovel with a small stream —
the culmination of a splintered history.

How To Find A Way

Come to the garden,
to lawns cloaked
in cypress and maple.

Under a tree,
lean into the morning,
the overhead branches
anchored in silence.

Rest a moment
as a caravan of cloud
dapples your face.

Take direction from shadow,
the shift of light as it turns.

Watch the orphan leaf
tossed from a branch
give movement to absence.

Bolton St. Memorial Park

Follow a raindrop's interior as it falls on stone,
entranced by that first dispersal of sound –
the dead cry their names
through a querulous October wind.

The Year of Our Lord, 1675

Beautiful cousin, I held you in my arms as an infant.
Freckles on your forehead reminded mother of a piebald,
father of Ursa Major – he tallied seven.

At an altar you smiled as our uncle thrust you forward,
your skin like vellum, a shadow of a blush on your cheek
flickered between candlelight dancing indifferent.

On our wedding night you cried, you missed your mother.
I consummated our union with a tale of a girl, her dead parents,
a greedy uncle, married at fifteen and her husband only seven.

Knead

Enough to start with,
a patchwork of shadows,

the morning light nudged
into this small corner of room

where the word knead rises in the air
and with it a small kitchen,

windows fogged
from the warmth of an oven.

I would watch the flick of her wrist,
the quick movement of her fingers

as she sprinkled flour on a tray,
her knuckles and hands
as they rolled and folded dough.

These days
I keep to familiar territory,

to a cloister of sky and rain,
finally emptied

just as the silver birch
I have watched for months,
is now lacquered and bare.

I return to the smoky blue
of a winter afternoon,

slipping into the corner of this room
as though a thief. Simple treasures —

the dew on the window
striated and veined,

the word knead
a child
pressing and folding within.

Solstice

In measured gains this path has become my own,
a slow ritual through bird song,
the hush of leaves skimmed along the road,
sunlight behind me as I walk.

On a day such as this, the weather
might change without word, and so
I return home, no Hestia there to warm
the hearth, only light shortening a fraction
through a window, tree shadows in flux.

Desert Road

Radio off, car doors swung open,
the crunch of footsteps on snow,
the soft bleating of lambs
staggering across the plains.

To the west
it is said there is no horizon –
this dark place of canyons and splintered scree
tumbling down from Mount Ruapehu.

On the road
a crackle of power lines surges the air,
snowdrift stiffens the sorrel back of the land
and the sun turns ghostly pearl.

Guarding the Flame

I will keep watch tonight,
lodged at the heel of Croghan hill
until tomorrow when it will be her turn.

The blush of a flame will keep me awake.
A vigil to sleep – the bruised sky,
cold winds sneaking round shadows like thieves.

I fall in and out of sleep,
smell the rain over the horizon,
listen to trees murmur as I move into dreams.

I meet my spirit on a road,
wandering without flesh or bone,
I ache as I see myself again,
a long time ago now, abandoned to this place.

Clouds stretch like fingers over the moon.
I yearn to be far from here, but sense her hand
on my shoulder like a small wing, white and faint.
Child she whispers to me – stay awake, stay awake.

Nora and Jim

I always said he should have given up
   the writing years ago. He was better
at singing my Jim. Though
    as he sleeps
   beside me in this hospital bed,

his eyes strange without their spectacles,
   hardly much use now, his sight
is almost gone. I remember

the cut of him the day we first met
  on Nassau St, himself
    only out of college
      and so mad with the world,
   full of fancy notions of how
he'd be the one to leave.

I didn't think he'd take me along,
    but he did –
Trieste, Paris, back to Dublin, Zürich…

I liked Trieste the best. It was where
  the two young ones were born.

And now no more.

I've lost many things in life.
   One still remains – my family name,
    Barnacle,
a sea creature with a hard shell,
   that's what Jim said.
Mostly, I think you find them
   on whales
  and after Nora,

even after all these years.

Rooms

From a sunlit window, you listen as keruru startle trees
and the wind rushes through the bush to God knows where.
Between the blow-in minors and rosellas you imagine
a kind of camaraderie, the understanding between immigrants.

So now we've had our introductions, let's cut to the chase,
steal beyond the hills, the unsealed roads, follow the flight path
of two continents, the world reduced to the back of a seat,
where if you close your eyes you'd find yourself walking
a rain-greyed street, your footsteps echoing a kind of silence
that finds dominion only in the after hours.

Given wings you'd look through the purple-shaded curtains
of your old apartment, hear the creak of the neighbours upstairs.
Even the art-deco woman painted on the door might whisper:
I know you, weren't you the one who left the African violet behind?

Every hour the veil moves back a little, memory is emboldened,
chancing itself, trying harder, trying too hard. Then to somewhere,
caught in the cold paper and echo of a room where you spent hours
watching the street, in search of the occupant of a taxi who'd left
months before, but you're getting ahead of yourself. First to another place:

the granite city of oil workers, short skirts, the toffee-coloured comfort
of Scottish malt, the vacuum of faux-parquet floors
repeating themselves endlessly. In winter
the walk to the shops, the long queue of solos,
their baskets filled with ready-made meals. Beautiful then,
the snow-covered avenues, the cold comfort seeping through your bones,
a grey sky holding itself for stories imagined in your kitchen,
the creaking gate in the garden a kind of taunt. What else could we say

for the revelations of rooms, places, sooner or later to be ignored,
and all too often seasonal like the circus, a kind of trapeze act
that dangles questions in the form of flexed muscle and tightened limb.

And what of the wind just now brushing through your life,
too far along its journey to be pushed aside, or when you awoke earlier,
dreams pressed on your tongue like ghosts, retreating over fields
and into those trees. Now you see it was no small thing to start here,

to do a double take, a kind of reversal through entrances and exits,
stretching as far as the eye can see, and if you could listen again
to the mutterings of words drifting through the door after you left that day,
those bereft rooms knew it would never be the same, and so you are here.

Notes

GUARDING THE FLAME – refers to one of the nineteen virgins who tended St Brighid's flame in Kildare. Brighid's sacred number was nineteen, representing the nineteen year cycle of the Celtic Year, the time it took from one new moon to the next to coincide with the Winter Solstice. It was believed though, that on the twentieth day of each cycle Brighid herself would tend the flame.

SIONNA – Irish goddess of the river Shannon and grand-daughter of Lir, the sea-god.

NIAMH – was married to Conall Caernach. While Cuchulainn was recovering from wounds in a battle, she nursed him and became his mistress. She then tried to prevent him from returning to battle. But Badb cast a spell on her so she wandered into the countryside. She then assumed the form of Niamh and told Cuchulainn to return to battle.

POHUTUKAWA – The Pohutukawa or Metrosideros (ironwood = hard timber) excelsa (tall) is one of the best known and most loved New Zealand native trees. Pohutukawa flowers are bright red, smothering the tree in December, hence its common name: the New Zealand Christmas Tree.

RURU – New Zealand owl, commonly known as the morepork; Ninox novaeseelandiae.

KERURU – New Zealand pigeon; Hemiphaga novaeseelandiae.

KAURI – New Zealand native tree, which can grow up to 50 metres with trunk girths of up to 16 metres, and live for more than 2000 years.

TUI – Prosthemadera novaeseelandiae. Native New Zealand bird.

PAEKAKARIKI – a seaside town, about 45 kilometres from Wellington.

BIRDLING'S FLAT – originally named Poranui, is located in Canterbury, South Island close to the shore of Lake Ellesmere.

PAPAGO – from the American Indian legend which tells of a Creator making butterflies from various elements in order to please children.

MAJELLA CULLINANE was born and raised in Ireland. She became a New Zealand resident in 2008, and lives on the Kapiti coast. She has previously received a Sean Dunne Young Writer's Award for Poetry, the Hennessy XO/Sunday Tribune Literary Award for Emerging Poetry and also an Irish Arts Council Award to study for an MLitt. in Creative Writing at St. Andrew's University Scotland. She has been a Writer in Residence in Ireland and Scotland.